Welcome to " Pills of Awakening" a journey undertaken with an open heart and a resolute mind. This volume is the fruit of an intimate spiritual awakening, written with passion and dedication by an Italian who wishes to share the precious experiences and realizations acquired along the way.

The author, compelled by the inner flame of their awakening, sought to convey in this book the valuable wealth of knowledge and insights accumulated. Through sincere writing and artistic expression, they dedicated themselves to translating the richness of their spiritual experience into tangible words.

The decision to personally translate this volume into English reflects the desire to overcome any linguistic barriers and share these wisdom pills with a broader audience. The author humbly acknowledges that, despite putting maximum effort into the translation, there might be nuances that fall short of linguistic perfection. Nevertheless, this does not diminish the determination to share the beauty and depth of the concepts learned during their own awakening journey.

In this journey, we apologize in advance to English-speaking readers if the language does not always reflect the perfection of everyday speech. The intention is to convey a message that transcends linguistic barriers, an invitation to explore one's awareness and embark on a journey of inner growth.

" Pills of Awakening " is more than a mere literary work; it is a passionate invitation to explore the richness of one's existence, embrace spiritual awakening, and share love and wisdom with the world. We hope that this literary experience also awakens your spirit, opening doors to deeper awareness and universal connection.

"Pills of Awakening" is an extraordinary journey in seven volumes, a path that will lead you through the intricacies of your consciousness and help you rediscover your connection with the universe. Each volume is a crucial milestone in this journey, designed to assist you in developing a deeper understanding of yourself and the world around you.

This series arises from the work of two minds, four hands, and two hearts transformed by a shared feeling and a profound desire for sharing what has been personally experienced. It cannot be withheld for oneself, as it rightfully belongs to every individual who feels and decides to deepen their self-knowledge. We will explore the roots of our state of spiritual slumber, shedding light on the cultural, social, and personal influences that have distanced us from our essential nature. We will begin to recognize the signs of spiritual awakening and understand why it is so vital for our emotional and spiritual well-being. It will be an immersion into the world of spiritual practic-

es, starting from meditation methods to mindfulness, from Eastern disciplines to Western practices. You will learn how these techniques can be integrated into your daily life to begin awakening your spirit. We will explore the nature of consciousness itself, seeking to answer profound questions such as: Who are we truly? What is our purpose in this world? Through self-reflection exercises and meditation, we will lay the foundations for a clearer understanding of ourselves and our path. We will tackle themes such as love, patience, compassion, gratitude, forgiveness, and connection with others.

Each volume will be enriched with stories of individuals who have experienced profound transformations through spiritual awakening, showing us that this journey is accessible to anyone with the will to explore it.

We will conclude our journey with a reflection on the meaning of spiritual awakening and how we can keep it alive in our everyday lives. It will be an invitation to live with mindfulness, to be present in every moment, and to cultivate a deep sense of gratitude for all that life has to offer.

These seven volumes are not just books but maps for an inner journey that can radically transform your life. I hope you can seize this opportunity to awaken your spirit and discover a new depth within yourself.
Safe travels!

Introduction to the concept of Spiritual Awakening

Conceptually, the term spiritual awakening refers to a process in which an individual gains greater awareness and a deepened connection with their inner and spiritual dimension.

This may involve a shift in perspective on life, increased compassion for others, a sense of inner peace, or a desire to explore deeper existential questions. Spiritual awakening can vary from person to person and may be triggered by various experiences, not always positive, such as moments of crisis, a search for meaning, or spiritual practice. These moments, sometimes even painful, are fundamental because it is the soul that calls for them to be able to listen to the path of awakening, traced even before birth, to which it is summoned to evolve and find awareness and true happiness. Therefore, when one senses a moment of change, it is necessary to listen and not be afraid to follow that intuition we feel inside like a faint voice amidst the clamor.

Spiritual awakening necessarily entails a significant shift in an individual's life perspective. This may manifest through a new understanding of personal values, increased awareness of connections among all things, a sense of gratitude for life, or a departure from material concerns in favor of a search for deeper meaning. Essentially, a change in perspective is a crucial element in the process of spiritual awakening. This shift in perspective during this process can take various forms, depending on the experiences and personal beliefs of each individual. Some common aspects of this change include:

1. *A sense of unity:*
Many people experience a sense of deeper connection with all individuals and with nature itself.
They see the world as interconnected and are concerned with preserving harmony and peace.

2. Change in values:

Priorities may shift from material desires to higher values such as compassion, love, truth, justice, and spirituality.

3. Increased awareness:

There is a heightened awareness of oneself, one's actions, and their impact on others. The focus is on personal and spiritual growth.

4. Search for meaning:

One begins to ask deeper questions about life, the meaning of existence, and one's personal mission. This search for meaning can lead to greater inner peace.

5. Less attachment:

There is a greater detachment from material concerns and a greater acceptance of the flow of life without resistance and attachment.

6. Inner peace:
Many people experience greater inner peace, a serenity that stems from trust in larger forces within the universe.

These are just some of the ways in which a shift in perspective can manifest in the process of spiritual awakening.

It is a highly individual journey and can vary significantly from person to person for various reasons:

1. *Background differences:*
   Past life experiences, culture, religion, and education of each individual influence their perspective on spirituality.
   These factors contribute to defining each person's unique awakening journey.

2. *Personal experiences:*
   Personal experiences, such as traumatic events, inner crises, moments of enlightenment, meaningful encounters, or inner

journeys, play a significant role in the process of spiritual awakening.

What can be a spark for one person may not be for another.

3. *Different Spiritual Approaches:*
There is a wide range of spiritual traditions and practices, each with its own philosophies and techniques. People may embark on different paths, such as Buddhism, Christianity, meditation, yoga, astrology, or even non-religious approaches, to explore their spirituality.

4. *Different Timings:*
Spiritual awakening can occur at various ages or stages of life.

Some may experience it at a young age, while others might come to it later in life, often in response to different challenges or inner questions.

It is important to know that during our earthly experience, the soul may have different moments, at different ages, when it is called to awaken. However, if lacking awareness or the courage to listen to intuition or the inner voice it feels, the process of awakening might not initiate and could be postponed to later in life. The call to awakening is for everyone, and it's not a train that passes only once; one just needs the courage to get on board and not linger too long at the station.

5. *Unique Goals:*
   Individuals may have different spiritual goals. Some seek inner peace, while others pursue wisdom, emotional healing, or spiritual growth.
   Some aspire to serve others and the community, or to be in harmony with nature and the Earth.

6. *Levels of Depth:*
   The depth and commitment to the spiritual path can vary significantly.
   Some may embrace rigorous daily practices, while others may have more occa-

sional experiences. The fundamental aspect, regardless of the depth, requires constancy and commitment because along the journey, obstacles and difficulties may be encountered, which can only be overcome with these qualities.

In conclusion, since each individual is unique with a combination of experiences, beliefs, and desires, the journey of spiritual awakening will always be different, unique, and unrepeatable for each person. It is a highly personal journey that reflects the diversity of the human condition, and such diversity should be regarded as a gift, an added value to this complex yet extraordinary path. Each individual carries a personal history of unique experiences, triumphs, challenges, and traumas. These experiences influence how a person perceives the world and navigates their spiritual journey. There are countless paths to spiritual awakening, and each path is uniquely charted for each of us.

It is possible that in some stretches, we share the journey with others because comparison can have constructive aspects, but fundamentally, the path is individual and personal.

As mentioned, some may follow a specific religious tradition, such as Buddhism or Islam, while others may choose more eclectic or non-religious approaches such as meditation or connection with nature.

The journey of awakening can evolve throughout a person's life.

Priorities, questions, and goals may change with age and experiences, leading to different phases of spiritual development. Changing goals or perspectives is not a negative aspect of personal growth as it is inherent in the path of evolution and thus in constant becoming. As mentioned earlier, some may dedicate their entire lives to spiritual development, engaging in daily practices, in-depth studies, and intense inner journeys, undertaking constant and demanding work. Others may take a lighter approach, dedicating only part of their time to spiritual exploration.

In any case, each person must choose the approach that feels most suitable for them, listening to oneself to clearly perceive which, among the many possibilities, is the best choice for their personal growth. Conceptions of God, spirit, or a higher power can vary significantly from person to person. Some may embrace a traditional deity, while others see spirituality as a connection to universal energy or an inner force.

Each individual seeks their own meaning and purpose in spirituality. For some, awakening may involve a quest for inner peace, while for others, it may mean active commitment to creating a better world through social action or compassion. Spiritual awakening often involves moments of profound transformation. These can often arise from intense experiences such as meditation and deep contemplation, or from confronting death, serving those less fortunate and in need, or having a mystical experience. Just because the path of spiritual awakening is a highly individual journey that reflects the diversity of the human condition, there is no "right" or "wrong" path, and everyone is free to explore their spirituality authentically, uniquely, and personally. What matters is the meaning and depth that a person finds in their spiritual journey and how it contributes to their well-being and connection with the world, the universe, the cosmos... with which one is, from birth, interconnected with everything and in everything.

The conception of man's interconnection with everything existing in the cosmos is a central element in many spiritual and philosophical traditions. This idea has various implications in the context of spiritual awakening:

Sensation of Unity:
Recognizing the interconnection with everything that exists can lead to a profound sense of unity with the universe. This sense of unity can be a goal in the spiritual awakening journey, as it fosters an experience of love, compassion, and empathy toward all forms of life.

Responsibility:
Interconnection can lead to increased awareness of the interdependence between humans, nature, and the entire planet. This can trigger a sense of

responsibility towards the environment, other living beings, and society as a whole.

Therefore, in daily practice, one may suddenly find themselves experiencing pain in the presence of any suffering of a living being, whether it be human, animal, or plant.

Search for Meaning:
The idea of being part of an interconnected cosmos can stimulate a deeper search for the meaning of existence. People may question how they fit into the broader fabric of the universe and their role in promoting harmony and awareness.

Transcendence of Selfishness:
Recognizing interconnection can help transcend selfishness and individualism. As a result, individuals may undergo a transformation where their selfish desires diminish in favor of a broader focus on collective well-being.

Meditation and Awareness:
Many spiritual paths, such as meditation and mindfulness practice, aim to directly experience interconnection. These practices facilitate and assist individuals in experiencing it through direct personal experience. In general, the idea of interconnection can be a significant catalyst for spiritual awakening, as it fosters a broader and more inclusive perspective on life and spirituality itself. However, it's important to emphasize that the perception of this state can vary from person to person and may be experienced in different ways during the spiritual awakening journey. The inner work on oneself is considered an essential path to the awakening of consciousness and the attainment of awareness. This journey is rooted in many spiritual and philosophical traditions and is supported by numerous anecdotal accounts of personal transformation, underscoring the importance of a genuine and sincere path of introspection within oneself as the foundation of the evolution of every human being, regardless of their religious belief or philosophical thought chosen to follow.

That's why inner work is considered so significant. It involves deep self-reflection, allowing for the exploration of one's beliefs, emotions, and behaviors.

This process helps identify and overcome mental blocks, past traumas, and negative patterns. Inner work promotes personal growth through self-improvement. This involves managing emotions, developing healthier relationships, and gaining greater self-confidence.

For this reason, often when embarking on this journey, there is a sense of inadequacy in places or with people with whom one used to feel comfortable. There begins a process of selection among friends and family, choosing places to frequent, especially avoiding crowded ones, as a preference for seeking silence and solitude or being with carefully chosen people develops.

Deep crises start to arise about everything that doesn't make one feel well and happy, including work and relationships. The journey indeed calls for profound changes that begin from the inner and spiritual realm but to be complete, they correspond to significant changes in the material realm as well, such as a sudden career change or a separation from a partner, or distancing oneself from toxic people—thoughts that have evidently been felt in the heart for a long time but never had the courage to face.

Spiritual awakening always has a material counterpart to fully manifest, requiring courage and taking responsibility for one's choices by stepping out of the comfort zone that provided an illusory sense of security for years creating a block to our evolution and personal growth to attain true happiness. Many believe that deep self-exploration can lead to experiential moments of spiritual enlightenment.

These experiences can involve a deeper connection with the divine or the nature of the universe. Inner work helps purify the mind and emotions from all negativity, fostering greater mental clarity and inner peace, which necessarily involves the use of meditation and mindfulness practices. These are powerful tools for self-work to develop self-awareness and connection with the surrounding world, helping overcome illusions and limited perceptions that hinder us from seeing reality more fully and clearly. As the attainment of awareness and the awakening of consciousness almost always represent different paths for each individual, it is important to remember that inner work is a process a demanding and non-linear process that requires time, dedication, and patience. Some may achieve quick results, while others might require years of practice and self-exploration. Therefore, while inner work is a potent path, it is also important to respect one's own pace and individual journey.

Each person is a unique individual carrying different experiences, challenges, and personal goals.

Respecting one's own pace allows for authentic self-work without feeling in competition or comparison with others. The process of inner work often involves the discovery of aspects of ourselves that may have been hidden or overlooked. Respecting one's own journey means accepting these discoveries without judgment or self-criticism and working on them gradually. This is why working on oneself can be emotionally intense and time-consuming. Respecting one's own pace helps prevent feeling overwhelmed or stressed by too many transformations happening simultaneously. Inner work is a long-term commitment. Respecting one's own pace allows for maintaining a consistent practice over time, making it sustainable and integrated into everyday life. It should not be replaced or eliminated by the spiritual work being pursued but rather coexist synergistically to create harmony, enabling daily life to shape itself around inner knowledge and resonate at the same vibration. Real change takes time and consistency.

By respecting one's own pace, it is more likely to achieve lasting improvements in one's life and awareness. It's important to be kind to oneself and honest about one's journey.

Respecting one's own timing doesn't indicate a lack of commitment but rather wisdom in recognizing that inner progress is a journey that deserves patience and care.

Self-Awareness

A deep understanding of oneself is a fundamental aspect to embark on a journey of inner and personal evolution.

This process of self-exploration is one of the keys to understanding who we are, what we want from life, and how we can achieve greater personal fulfillment. Below, we will explore the importance of self-knowledge in initiating a path of inner evolution.

Self-awareness begins with an understanding of what we are and how we react to situations, emotions, and internal and external stimuli.

This awareness is the starting point for making positive changes in our lives. Without it, we might continue to repeat the same mistakes or harmful behaviors, getting stuck in a process of stereotypes and automatism that give us the illusion of living in reality but have actually only hindered us in our path of awakening and evolution. Knowing oneself involves recognizing one's abilities, talents, and passions.

These strengths can be leveraged to pursue meaningful personal and professional goals. Knowing what we are good at allows us to make the most of our potential.

In addition to acknowledging strengths, self-awareness also means accepting one's weaknesses and flaws. This acceptance not only makes us more humble but also provides an opportunity to work on them and strive to improve, reaching the best version of ourselves. Self-awareness helps improve relationships with others, as the perception of our inner world in its complexity directly results in understanding others. When we better understand our needs, values, and boundaries, we can communicate more effectively and constructively, thereby reducing conflicts and misunderstandings. Truly knowing oneself helps establish life goals that are authentic and meaningful. When we are aware of our true aspirations and desires, we can focus our energies on what truly matters to us and work towards achieving those goals.

One of the most effective methods to begin self-discovery is self-exploration, which involves introspection into the deepest part of ourselves—a process that is constantly evolving.

As we grow and change, it is important to continue gaining self-awareness to adapt to new circumstances and phases of life.

We can affirm, therefore, that self-awareness is a deep and ongoing process that often leads to greater personal fulfillment, happiness, and success in life.

This process requires introspection, self-reflection, and openness to personal growth. The journey of inner evolution begins with a desire — the desire to discover who we truly are and to live a more authentic and meaningful life. This desire is the key to initiating all stages of the spiritual awakening journey, as it is such a powerful inner drive that leads to significant and authentic changes. There are many exercises that can help increase self-awareness and kickstart a path of spiritual evolution.

However, it is important to note that everyone may have different experiences and needs, so it is crucial to find exercises that best suit one's own situation. Some helpful examples, aimed at addressing this inner desire and aiding in the journey of self-awareness, could include:

Meditation;
Journaling;
Mindfulness;
Yoga;
Gratitude Practice;
Spiritual Studies;
Inner Dialogue.

Now, let's try to clarify what these practices really involve, without being overly verbose and allowing the reader the opportunity to be drawn to one practice over another, fostering curiosity to explore the topic further on their own. After all, if you've come this far in reading, it's likely because you feel within yourself that desire to learn, know, and engage in practices that you (and your soul) are drawn to for evolutionary needs that have emerged.

Meditation

Meditation teaches to become aware of one's thoughts, emotions, and physical sensations. Through consistent practice, you learn to observe yourself objectively, without judgment.
This self-awareness is crucial for spiritual development as it allows you to explore your inner self deeply. Practicing it regularly can lead to a sense of inner peace and serenity. Through practice, you learn to manage stress, anxiety, and daily concerns, which is helpful in freeing the mind to explore deeper spiritual issues. It can assist you in connecting with your inner dimension. Many spiritual traditions teach that inner truth and connection with the divine can be found through stillness and contemplation. Meditation provides a means to open the door to this spiritual connection. During meditation, you can begin to explore profound questions about life, meaning, morality, and your purpose. This process of self-exploration can lead to greater clarity about who you are and what you seek in your evolution. It teaches you to observe your feelings

without automatically reacting to them. This provides you with greater mastery over your emotions, allowing you to manage them in a healthier and more constructive way.

It can increase your empathy and compassion for others.

When you develop greater self-awareness, you become more attuned to the needs and sufferings of others, thereby contributing to your spiritual development. Meditative practices teach you to transcend the ego, moving beyond identification with the separate "self" and experiencing a sense of unity with the universe or a broader spiritual dimension. This is a continuous path of spiritual growth and development.

As you practice regularly, you will discover new inner depths and refine your connection with the universe.

Journaling

Journaling, or personal diary writing, is a powerful practice that can be extremely helpful in spiritual and evolutionary development.
Writing about oneself and one's journey requires introspective reflection.
You can explore profound questions about life, meaning, morality, and your relationship with the divine. This reflection can lead to greater clarity and self-awareness on important spiritual and personal matters. Practicing it allows you to explore your emotions in detail.
You can examine how you feel in certain situations or regarding certain aspects of your spiritual life. This emotional exploration can help you better understand yourself and manage your emotions in a healthy way.
 It can help you document your spiritual journey over time, providing awareness of the changes you are making even in similar or recurring situations. You can record your spiritual experiences, moments of insight, and progress in your development. This allows you to trace your path

and see how you have grown over time. It can also be a means of creative expression. You can write poems, aphorisms, philosophical thoughts, or even draw and paint in your journal. This creative expression can help you explore and uniquely communicate your experiences. At times, you may encounter obstacles or blocks in your evolutionary spiritual journey. Writing about these blocks can help you identify them and find ways to overcome them. You can examine your fears, uncertainties, pains, or inner resistances and work through them. You can use your journal to plan your journey in its various stages.

You can set goals and objectives, plan daily practices, track progress, and make plans for the future.

After significant spiritual experiences, such as meditations, dreams, or meaningful encounters, you can write about these experiences to integrate them into your understanding of yourself and your spiritual journey.

Journaling is a personal and flexible activity, so you can tailor it to your needs and preferences.

You can write in a structured or freeform manner, on a daily or sporadic basis.

The important thing is that journaling becomes a tool for self-exploration and evolutionary development, helping you grow and develop a deeper understanding of yourself and your spiritual path. In this regard, at the end of this volume, we have deliberately left blank pages that can be used to begin experimenting with this practice.

Mindfulness

Mindfulness is a practice that involves being aware of the present moment deliberately and without judgment. It can be extremely helpful in evolutionary and spiritual development in various ways. It teaches us to be present in the current moment, rather than being distracted by the past or worried about the future. The "Live here and now" allows you to experience reality as it is, which is crucial not only for many spiritual traditions but also because it represents the masterful way to be present with oneself in everyday life. This provides a means to attain self-awareness, which only living in the present can offer. Indeed, no one has the power to change their past, nor can they predict the future. However, "Living here and now" allows us to correct who we are today as a result of our past and to direct our future with positive, authentic, and mindful thought forms, giving the right value to the present, which is our only certainty. In this way, mindfulness helps us to become more aware of ourselves, our thoughts, our emotions, and our reactions.

This self-awareness is an important step in spiritual development as it allows us to explore and better understand our inner selves. Often, the mind is constantly occupied by thoughts, worries, and mental noise. Mindfulness teaches us to calm the mind and reduce the continuous and incessant flow of thoughts, allowing us to experience moments of inner peace. It helps us manage emotions in a healthier way. Instead of reacting impulsively to emotions, we learn to observe them without judgment, which can lead to greater emotional stability. The consistent practice of mindfulness teaches us acceptance and compassion, both towards ourselves and others.

This aspect is often central to evolutionary and spiritual development, as it encourages us to treat ourselves and others with kindness and love. For many people, mindfulness is a means to develop a deeper connection with the divine or a spiritual dimension.

Practicing it can foster spiritual experiences, such as moments of transcendence or a sense of unity with oneself and the universe. It is a continually evolving practice.

Even after years, there is always something new to discover about oneself and one's innermost being and spirituality. This leads to continuous and exponential personal growth, contributing to greater inner peace and serenity, which can be particularly helpful for those seeking balance and harmony in their spiritual life.

To develop mindfulness, it's important to practice it regularly. You can do this through mindfulness meditation, body scan, awareness during daily activities such as eating or walking, and other mindfulness techniques.

Remember that mindfulness practice takes time and patience, but it can have a profound impact on your evolutionary and spiritual development and your overall quality of life.

A couple of practical examples for this practice could be:

Exercise 1

Mindful Breathing:

Find a quiet and comfortable place to sit or lie down.

Close your eyes and focus your attention on your breath.

Notice the movement of the breath as it enters and exits your body.

Pay attention to the sensation of air passing through your nostrils, the movement of your chest or abdomen.

When the mind wanders (and it will), gently bring your attention back to the breath, without judgment.

Continue for 10-20 minutes.

Exercise 2

Mindful Eating:

Prepare a healthy meal or snack.

Sit at a table without distractions such as TV or a cellphone.

Observe the food attentively, noticing colors, smells, and textures.

Savor each bite of the meal slowly, focusing on the taste and texture of the food. Be aware of how the food satisfies your body and hunger.

This exercise helps you connect with your body and appreciate food more fully.

Exercise 3

Mindful Walking:

Go to a quiet and peaceful place for a slow walk.

Focus on the movements of your feet as you walk. Feel the contact of your feet with the ground, the lifting, and lowering.

Pay attention to the sounds, smells, and sensations around you.Walk without a specific destination, simply experiencing the act of walking.

This exercise helps you be fully present in your walking experience.

Exercise 4

Short Mindfulness Break:

At any point during the day, take a short break.

Try closing your eyes for a moment and take a deep breath.

Notice the physical sensations, emotions, and thoughts you are experiencing in that specific moment. Welcome everything that comes without judgment.

This exercise can be done even in everyday situations to regain presence at any time. Remember that the key to mindfulness is kindness toward yourself and regular practice.

As you develop your ability to be present with yourself, you can experience greater awareness, tranquility, and well-being in your life.

Yoga is an ancient practice rooted in the spiritual traditions of India. It is based on the idea that the mind, body, and spirit are interconnected, and through the harmony of these three elements, one can achieve a state of total well-being. This practice leads you to become more aware of your body.

Through the postures (asanas) and movements, you learn to feel physical sensations, discover any tensions, and work on them.

This body awareness is a crucial step in spiritual development as it allows you to connect with yourself on a deeper level, encourages mind control through concentration on breath and attention to the present moment. This is fundamental in many spiritual traditions, as a calm and focused mind is considered a vehicle for the discovery of deeper spiritual truths. Yoga seeks to create a balance between the mind, body, and spirit. This balance contributes to a sense of inner harmony and well-being, which can support spiritual growth. By practicing it, you can explore your inner world. Moments of silence and introspection during the practice can lead to a deeper understanding of yourself, your emotions, and your thoughts. It can serve as a path to develop a deeper spiritual connection.

Yoga practices often include meditations, mantras, and prayers, which can help establish a connection with the divine or a broader spiritual dimension. It is a journey of continuous personal growth.As you practice regularly, you will discover new aspects of yourself and your spiritual development.

You can progress through different levels of practice and refine your understanding of your inner world, promoting greater inner peace and serenity. This can be particularly helpful for those seeking balance and harmony in their spiritual life. It is important to note that this discipline is a highly individual practice and can be adapted to your needs and goals. It is not necessary to be flexible or have a specific religious belief to practice yoga. You can choose the style and level of practice that best suits you and your journey.

The key is consistency and openness to personal and evolutionary growth.

The Practice of Gratitude

The practice of gratitude is a habit that involves deliberately focusing on what one is grateful for in one's life.

This practice can be extremely helpful in spiritual and evolutionary development in various ways. It helps you concentrate on the positive aspects of your life, even when facing challenges and difficulties.

This positive perspective can significantly enhance your quality of life and spiritual well-being. It invites you to pay attention to the details of your daily life, encouraging you to notice the small things that often go unnoticed.

This increased awareness can lead you to be more present and connected with the current moment, a key component of evolutionary and spiritual development. Practicing gratitude can bring about a sense of humility.

Recognizing the blessings and opportunities you have in life can help you understand how fortunate you are and develop a sense of humility towards the world and others.

We often focus on what is lacking in life, which can lead to feelings of dissatisfaction and emptiness. The practice of gratitude helps you see and appreciate what you already have, thereby reducing dissatisfaction and excessive desire for more. Gratitude can make you more empathetic and compassionate.

When you acknowledge your blessings, you tend to develop a greater understanding of others and be more open to sharing your time, resources, and affection. Expressing gratitude towards others strengthens social bonds and interpersonal relationships.These connections can be crucial for your spiritual development as they can provide emotional as well as spiritual support. Additionally, it can help you develop emotional resilience. When facing tough and challenging times, awareness of your past blessings can give you the strength to overcome current challenges. Remembering oneself and what one has been

able to achieve in the past, especially in difficult moments, is different from dwelling on the past. Remembering oneself in this case allows us to be grateful for what we have been and have accomplished, giving us the courage to face present challenges because we are aware of our qualities and human and spiritual worth. You can incorporate the practice of gratitude into your daily life by noting things you are grateful for, reflecting on them, or expressing this gratitude to others.
This practice can be adapted to your lifestyle and personal preferences; however, it is essential to do it regularly to maximize the spiritual benefits.

Spiritual Studies

Spiritual studies are an essential part of the path of spiritual and evolutionary development. They involve the exploration and deepening of matters related to spirituality, religion, and the quest for deeper meaning in life.

They allow you to gain a deeper understanding of your spiritual traditions or the traditions of other cultures.

This can lead to increased awareness of spiritual practices, beliefs, and history. Many people seek answers to profound existential questions, such as the meaning of life, the nature of the universe, or the role of humans in the cosmic order. Spiritual studies often provide perspectives and answers to these questions and can help you develop a much deeper and authentic personal spirituality. You can explore practices and beliefs that resonate with you and aid in your spiritual growth. They may teach you meditation and prayer practices that can lead to moments of profound spiritual connection. These practices can help you find a sense of inner peace and develop a relationship with the divine, including an ethical and moral component.

This can help you develop a sense of responsibility and compassion toward others, which are fundamental aspects of spiritual development, and lead you to explore different religious and spiritual traditions.

This open-mindedness can enrich your understanding and foster tolerance and empathy toward diverse perspectives. This, too, is a path of continuous growth. As you deepen your understanding through these studies, you may discover new aspects of yourself and the world around you.

To derive the maximum benefit from these studies, it is important to have an open mind, genuine curiosity, and a respectful approach to diverse traditions.

You can explore these studies through reading, participating in study groups, meditation, prayer practice, or through the guidance of spiritual leaders or mentors. Remember that your spiritual journey is a personal and unique one, and studies can help you find your meaning in life. Even the reading you are engaging in today is a tangible start to your study.

Inner Dialogue

Inner dialogue is a practice in which a person engages in conscious dialogue with oneself.

It may involve an internal conversation to explore thoughts, emotions, beliefs, and personal values. This type of dialogue can be extremely beneficial for spiritual and evolutionary development.

This practice provides an opportunity to explore the depths of onc's inner self.

You can inquire about who you are, what you believe, what your values and spiritual goals are, and what meaning you attribute to your life.

This process of self-exploration can lead to greater self-awareness and awareness of your spiritual journey. Through inner dialogue, you can examine complex spiritual issues. You can explore your beliefs about the nature of the universe, the divine, or the meaning of life. This reflection can lead to a deeper understanding of your spiritual beliefs. It can help you manage your emotions in a healthier way.

You can examine your emotional reactions to specific events or situations and seek to better understand them. This emotional awareness can be valuable for your evolutionary development, as emotions often play a significant role in this process. Sometimes, there are internal conflicts or moral dilemmas that require resolution. Inner Dialogue allows you to explore both sides of a dilemma and seek a solution that is in harmony with your spiritual values.

It contributes to developing a stronger personal ethical foundation. You can examine what you consider right or wrong and how you want to live your life based on these beliefs. For some people, it is a means of communicating with the divine or with the Higher Self.

This may include prayer, meditation, or simple internal conversations with a spiritual presence.

This type of dialogue can lead to meaningful spiritual experiences.

Through it, you can develop a plan or even a personalized spiritual practice.

You can set spiritual goals, plan rituals or daily practices, and track your progress over time. It can lead you to be more aware of the present moment, helping you learn to live with greater presence and attention, which is crucial for many spiritual traditions.

To practice inner dialogue, you can find a quiet place and dedicate time to reflect and write or think about the spiritual questions and themes you want to explore. You can do this regularly as part of your spiritual development routine or when you feel the need for answers or to explore deep issues. The important thing is to be open, honest, and kind to yourself during this process.

Conclusions

In the conclusion of this first volume of "Awakening Pills" (more will follow in continuation of this), the essential elements that make it an extraordinarily enlightening work emerge, where the author intentionally guides the reader to explore the possibility of an intimate journey within the human mind and heart, revealing the multiple and complex facets of self-awareness. Through a pragmatic narrative and in-depth research, the author emphasizes the importance of looking within ourselves to discover the truth about our nature, emotions, and thoughts, highlighting the power of self-awareness as a tool for personal growth, transformation, and the realization of authentic authenticity.

The intention is to provide valuable insights and practical teachings on how to develop self-awareness, using meditations, introspective exercises, and inspiring stories of individuals who have transformed their lives through this process. Of this, you can only be proud because it means that you are preparing, or rather, your Soul is preparing you, to initiate a new process within you through which it will show you not only the wonder of creation but above all what a splendid and marvelous creature you truly are.

So, all that remains is for you to start following your instincts and begin to trust more in its intuitions, choosing the beginning of your path that will bring to light the true you.

My Journaling...

Index